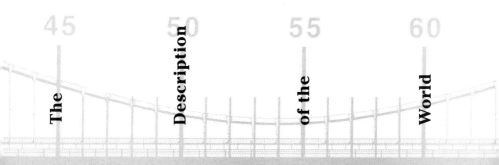

The Description of the World

Johanna Skibsrud
# The Description of the World

A Buckrider Book

Buckrider Books is an imprint of Wolsak and Wynn Publishers.

Cover images © owik2, aremac / photocase.com
Cover and interior design: Natalie Olsen, Kisscut Design
Author photograph: Dan Davis
Typeset in Chronicle Text and ITC Cheltenham
Printed by Coach House Printing Company Toronto, Canada

 Canada Council   Conseil des Arts
for the Arts   du Canada

 Canadian   Patrimoine
Heritage   canadien

 ONTARIO ARTS COUNCIL
CONSEIL DES ARTS DE L'ONTARIO
an Ontario government agency
un organisme du gouvernement de l'Ontario

The publisher gratefully acknowledges the support of the Canada Council for the Arts, the Ontario Arts Council and the Canada Book Fund.

Buckrider Books
280 James Street North
Hamilton, ON
Canada L8R 2L3

Library and Archives Canada Cataloguing in Publication
Skibsrud, Johanna, 1980–, author
The description of the world / Johanna Skibsrud.
Poems.
ISBN 978-1-928088-21-9 (paperback)
I Title.
PS8587.K46D48 2016      C811'.54      C2016-905409-8

*For John*

# Contents

I

# I

Dream a narrowing; dream: a clenched fist, a hollow.

Dream blood, now; dream bones.

Dream flesh for bones, and veins for blood to travel.

Let each dreamed thing become that thing.

Let each grow, inside you.

Let each split you into minute, unfathomable parts; a
great mystery for ten thousand future generations
slowly to unravel.

Dream lungs now; dream the very first breath.

Dream hands. Dream eyes.


Now dream sight for eyes, and hit it – like a wall.

Let there be no way around it, this time.


Let eyes *see* sight, and know it is a wall.

Dream a small hole in the wall the eyes have made.


Dream the hole is a door the hands can open.

**II**

Draw a single moment. As it begins – slowly at first,
then all at once – to accept the given parameters, give up
everything it is not.

Draw, for example, the way you woke up this morning.

The way everything was vague; the objects of the room inseparable
at first from the shifting objects of your mind.

The way they only gradually took on recognizable form –
but that once they did, it was as though they had always existed
that way.

And there was no other possible configuration for the distances
between your body, say, and mine.

No other possible angle for the light streaming in through the open
door – or for the one green stalk of the mostly dead plant,
to which we continue to grant its daily allotment of water,
though we know that it will die.

As though life really existed in single moments – such as this one.

In which we breakfast together in the yard, complaining of how
late it has already become.

As though there was actually a way that we could slip behind.

As though we were not already, in being at all, existing also in
some other way – alien even to ourselves – in our own backyard,
at our own breakfast table.

**III**

When, after the thought has been pressed to its point,
to become the field that extends itself past the line of the
horizon, have the heart extend itself – a further field, beyond
that one.

## Brief Sketches of an Open Field

Trees take shape on the horizon
not as what they are, but against
what they are not.

Everything bends for a moment,
then levels itself, then bends.

*

As the foot of a snail inside its shell,
the shell not knowing, and the foot not knowing –

so the mind – a landscape, cleared of form –
erects three trees,

has already beheld them.

*

What remains difficult, when, as now, thoughts wing themselves
across an empty field, scattering in all directions,
is not to erect again: a fence, a branch, a wire,

for them to scatter to, then rest upon.

*

II

## Maestro Bartolomé Reconsiders his *Creation of Eve.*

Sometime, late in the fifteenth century, Maestro Bartolomé gazed
out, to where – across the empty square and slanted rooftops of
the city – the spires of a distant cathedral struck the sky.

There is always that inevitable point, he thought, where the visible
is no longer split into seen and unseen, and the unseen simply
drops away into a further unseen.

If he could paint *that.*

Not woman as she was in the moment – or just after – having
emerged from the man, but the way that she arrives –

is always arriving –

unannounced and utterly new, from what – beyond what can be
apprehended and named: "unseen," "unknown" – simply is that thing.

If he could paint *that.* Woman as landscape. But beyond both the
limit and the idea of landscape.

If he could paint just: a blur of colour and form, a collapsed line
indicating where line can no longer be drawn...

Woman as the emergency of every moment, arriving
unaccountably from some place beyond the imagined limit of itself.

And love, too...

If he could paint *love* as both the emergence and dissolution of
every form...

And so creation, the issue of love, as that which (rather than being applied simply, in layers) arises always as if independent of the hand of the artist who drew it there, in the form of chance: a pure gift.

As that which merely glances – suddenly, and without direction – off the surface, as light glances off of water. Or as one density of air glances off of another – creating, as it does so, a current of wind.

The Maestro turned back to his painting.

I've missed nothing! He thought. Creation itself is only just now occurring! Is just *about to occur.*

He picked up his brush and held it for a breathless moment in the air.

Then he painted out the woman; he painted out the man.

Then – as best he could – he drew man and woman at once –

so it was impossible to tell any longer which form emerged from which, and both and neither hesitated

just as his brush had hesitated, a moment ago, in the air.

## "Come and See the Blood in the Streets!"

As the form of a flame. Less form than flame.

As bells, as clocks, as trees... As a shout,
a held breath. As the bursting of geraniums...

The world enters, intrudes. Becomes, again,
what it already was.

The thought precedes it as a hand precedes the word –
only afterward leaving its mark.

So that even if, in being drawn against that distance,
an explanation fails; is only this: a line, so brief as to be
invisible to the eye – as that behind an ascending bird,
which is, in the moment of its seeing, already gone...

Then it is that. Or at least the question left in that wake.

Beyond, there is just – a sheet of light against the sky.

As Pablo Neruda once wrote: "All the blood of the children
ran through the streets like the blood of children," as literal
as that.

As though a thought, derived from no source, had, at every
moment, already emerged.

The heart pierced through, the question trailing.

## The Abstract Figure Dreams of His Release

To be lain diagonal across that long distance!

To glide, undetected, on the slouched shoulders of the
quietly pacing museum guard.

To approach; be recognized. Not as finally human,
finally real, but instead, as a simple line, a narrowing.

What will eyes and ears look like then? When there is no
shape that eyes and ears have taken? What noise will
sound make when even the muted step of the museum guard
is stilled?

What shape will love take, when there is no longer any
distance between us, and my long shadow, on your long shadow,
only falls and falls?

## I Give My Powers Away

I used to creep out past the gates at night,
to stand alone in darkness.

I was singular then, as though driven
to the earth.

Returning, I would lie again beside the fire –
hold the shelf of my shoulder blade in one hand,
like a knife.

But still my throat, my lungs, those empty things,
would be out there on the plain.

Still gaping, still swallowing things.

## They Will Take My Island

Soon, they will dismantle the fish, the banana stands.

For a long time now, the hotel bar at the end of the pier has stood vacant and closed.

The far point, from where on so many nights I stood, watching the lights of the night fishermen – soon even that will sink from view.

And my own house. It, too, will be lifted from the root, so that only four round stumps, beneath it, will remain. Each one so remote from the form they bore, and from each other, that they will dream that they are trees, bearing only emptiness between them.

I will climb to the highest point – wait for the water to rise.

For the lights of the fishermen to blink out, one by one, like stars – long after the fishermen have all been drowned.

Then, I, too, will be slowly dismantled.

My skull – through which once, as above the stuccoed walls, the brass band played – emptied, my heart picked clean from its root,

and the four corners of my body at last so remote from one another that they, too, will dream that they are trees,

emptiness no more an emptiness between them.

## Everything in the World is Open

Everything in the world is open.

There is nothing hidden,
no secret impulse; nothing

ravenous, as the appetite
of history, at the core.

No, there is nothing at the core.

Everything is here. Is open.
Is waiting to be known.

Even the centre –
so long adrift as to be
finally irrelevant,

and language, too.

This is the gift. This is the only
offering.

It is not too much.

Despite or because of this.

Everything still exists – still
holds. There is no single

way of pronouncing it.

## Sestina

The fields below the house still open on the wild,
though I've travelled to their limit many times by now, and past,
and seen the way that distance opens only onto further distance,
and there is never any end. There remains, there must remain (unseen –
perhaps unknown), a simple given. An absolute. This same field,
for example, but from the perspective of a squirrel

or of a star, does not simply disappear. Though for the squirrel,
too vast, for the star, too small, there persists, the "opening," the "wild."
The seeing, that is, does not alter the thing that's seen, or make the field
less prone to distances – to limits one cannot think past.
Just as the poem exists despite the poem. Unheard, unseen –
"as if" unknown: the near thing the words are always hunting in
    the distance

after; the far thing against which the poem – "the field" – is understood
    as distance.
How might I begin to gaze at my own life as if I were a squirrel
or were a star? To see the way that it remains, from that perspective,
    unlived, unseen –
That there exists no "opening," no "limit"? That all, instead, is formless,
    wild?
That though words, like points of view, fall short, or are flung well past
the thing they seek to name or see, it makes no difference to the field?

It is in always somewhat missing its mark that the field, after all,
    becomes the field.

That it emerges against its limit – that final edge – to take its shape
    as distance.
How might words, I wonder, stretch at last, and all the way down?
    Finally past
that edge? Toward where the field gives way to what, beyond the field,
    the squirrel
and star agree, *exists* – not just as an idea, but as what is simple, open, wild?
To where distance finally falls away to become the mere rattle of a nut –
    unseen

in its shell? Even the wild realizable, when held in hand. Though unseen,
it, too, exists. It, too, is contained – yes – like a nut in a shell. Or like a field
inside of a field. Creating the distance: the idea of the "opening," the "wild."
Creating the distance, that is to say, through and as a result of distance.
And is there any other way? Of speaking of the field, without also of the
    squirrel
and of the star? Of simply *seeing* the field without falling short or seeing past

that which, because of or despite the field the field simply *is*? Is there a past
or a falling short of what remains – beyond the field – unseen?
A way to see or speak of distance without merely leaping like a squirrel
branch to branch, without pausing to ask if sight or speech will hold?
    Is the field
merely an attempt to speak of the way that, via distance, we arrive
    at distance?
That, via "openings" we close in on – and thus close out – what's wild?

For we leap (don't we?) always precisely to the limit, never past.
    The field
is always taking shape, unseen, in the shape of a field. Becoming,
    again, the distance
a squirrel closes in a single bound, a star opens as against itself:
    what's still unseen, what's wild.

## The Description of the World

Like language, love is the desire not to be a simple illustration,
but to be instead –

and continuously – a "starting out" across distances that have not
yet been, and may never be drawn.

It is the hope that "you," toward whom "I" intend to travel, will
recognize in what, in truth, is just a smudge or a tear on a nearly
empty page, the form of a bridge, or a boat –

and within or upon that form, the form a woman – and within or
upon that form, "me."

When there is no reason for you to do so.

When it could equally be a simple mistake, made by the artist,
or by chance, or by time…

When it could still be so many things. A wave, for example.
A bird, a whale –.

No, it does not have to be me out there, drifting.

Across uncharted waters, on an unseen breeze.

IV

## In the Dream, It Shows

The moment, once opened, unfurled, like a map or a fan, creates the impression of a single thing.

As if movement was a thing; as if repetitiveness, as if becoming used to things as they are was a thing.

The eye tracks it. If the eye does not track it, the mind tracks it. If the mind does not, the soul. The soul senses it, and if the soul does not, or if there is no soul, if the soul is only a way of speaking of the heart, or the heart the mind, or the mind, a certain separateness of things –.

Or, if the mind is the thing –.

If the saying of things is only a naming of the mind, which approaches the thing, not as it appears to the eye, but as it, in turn, approaches itself –.

There is, in any case, the thing.

Its progress broken into component parts; each not an object, but a longing, and each longing within each part a real thing.

Even the eye, then, a longing. For all things to unfold, to spread themselves before the mind.

To become the thing chosen, ventured upon by the body.

For time itself to erupt against that limit; to become the first wish – itself, an unfurling –.

As a seed spins upward; as the seed of a flower gone white overnight spins upward – suspends itself; climbs; is borne on air.

Now the words begin to crowd in, the way they do at the edges of dreams, when there is, into the dream, the first hint of waking.

When consciousness becomes the cloud that covers the field that the thinking breaks.

Images pushed back – a sudden emptiness of bones.

Flight, already, an afterthought.

## Introduction to Repetition

At first: silence.

A first, hard edge against which we began to conceive, and then to measure, the listenable, the heard.

Within which measure we discovered the inertia of interval. A distance not from one point to the next, but something deeper, internal to the structure.

A distance that was, before the animal, the shape of the animal, the invisible branching of a first nuclei.

That erupted not as a question, requiring a response, but instead as the interruptive shout, resulting at its edges and for the first time in a knowledge of and thus a longing for origin.

That, in establishing itself as both a fixed and fallible point, at or beyond the periphery: *unheard, unknown*, begat the shout, which broke, in a single, indiscernible, beat, the steady drone of the solid heart;

which exploded the sun, and rained down, in intervals, the earth upon the earth;

which gave birth to words, and repeated itself, endlessly, until the words, too, took the shape of the earth – became it.

Until the earth – in slow, unsteady, affirmation – pressed against itself, and pressing, wore down its highest peaks, exhausted its oceans –.

## The Real is That Which Always
## Comes Back to the Same Place

For the thought to exist singly, as for itself. For distances
to collapse, be made arable, assembled in rows –

along which one might even travel, unhindered, and from
that perspective begin to see the way that the farthest
visible point from the thought itself is not a limit, but only
the point at which the thought, extending itself infinitely
in that direction, encounters itself.

For it to become the sudden violence of that encounter.
A legion of scattered forces, already begun at a charge.
A final, continuous, attempt to take the last line.

Not to hold it, now, but to destroy it utterly. For them to have
already plunged themselves into whatever of the words, or of the
thought, outside of themselves, which had, in the first place,
ordered them to industry or war, can be made flesh, bear contact.

For them to have already turned and fled. Tearing at their clothes
– at their own skins – at the wounds they, themselves, inflict there.

Until there is nothing to tear, until even the thought is gone, and
will not now rise, and had not then risen.

## The Other, Already There

One sensed it, even as a child.

When – climbing into the highest branches of the tree in the yard
– one glimpsed the earth from that distance, and one's own
position, relative to it. And understood.

The weight of the body, in accordance to that distance.

Was held by it, and knew it was that by which it was held. Knew
that if there was a fixed point, it would be that:

The cause and also the effect of the illusion that all of this is
something with which one might actually come into proximity.

Knew that one might, in keeping absolutely still – in
acknowledging the fragility of the weight-bearing
crook of the tree within which one's perspective is fixed and held,
like a stone in crosshairs, prepared to be fired –

one might, without the tension ever actually being released, sail
toward that point; which is to say, one might *never have to
choose*; might remain forever, poised above the earth, even when
evening comes and the light from the porch blinks on and
everyone else has long ago scattered indoors – while at the same
time, descending, descending.

Toward the voice that calls, the warmth indoors,
the meal already laid.

V

## At Last, the Poet Returns to the City

At last, the poet returns to the city.

Nobody recognizes her; nobody knows she has returned.

She watches the people come and go, bringing their goods to the
marketplace.

Now a blind man walks by and recognizes the poet.

"Ah," he says, "so you've returned.

"It was for your own good that we sent you away. Now everything
is as it appears; you need not speak any longer in riddles or tongues."

The people gather round. They build a table for the poet, and they
sit the poet at the table.

"Now, the poet will defend herself."

"Do you swear" – the blind man asks, raising his right hand – "to
fasten each word only to what is solid and true?

"That – though man is rarely of one mind and is, therefore, often
at war with himself – you will lead him, so far as you are able,
toward reason and law, away from conflict, indeterminacy and
unnecessary suffering?"

The poet opens her mouth to reply, but no sound comes.

Even the blind man sees that there is nothing to see.

No difference, finally, between silence and law, darkness and light.

Confused, the people cry out: "what possible meaning is there in any of this?"

But their words break on their tongues, and gather like stones at their feet.

Someone picks up a stone.

He slams his fist onto the table the people have built, and throws the stone at the poet.

The people cheer and shout. Every cheer turns to a stone at their feet.

The people pick up the stones. They beat on the table with their fists and throw their stones at the poet.

The table shatters. The poet flees.

The people sit in the ruined agora.

They pick up the pieces of the table they had built.

"I thought this was a table," they say, "but how can it be a table if it shatters at a single blow?

"How can it be a table if it is only this part?"

VI

## Flying Home Aboard Enola Gay

Afterward, only the loneliness of ordinary moments, nothing more.

Save, perhaps: a constriction of the throat.

A sudden abhorrence of the way that, despite or because of single moments: the way each loses itself, irreversibly, in becoming the next, everything continues.

A sudden abhorrence of number and language – the flimsy instruments used.

## Incident aboard the *Lucky Dragon:* March 1, 1954

To name is to press what is
into the shape of what also is.

The idea: a perfect cylinder.

Extending only so far, and not past.

As a hand reaches only so far –
never past – the object that it grasps.

A contact across two distances forced into being
not through difference
but by the slow accretion of the same.

Never anything but the result.

The impossibility of any naming of
the "there is" of "there is."

For this reason, it is absolutely imperative
that language be general.

That the act of nomination should
consume itself, *indicating nothing*.

That it be only its own description: "at first
a flash, a yellow light."

That it be a "Wondering what happened," a
"jump[ing] up from the bunk near the door,
[running] out on deck."

That it be: "astonished." Be:

"Bridge, sky, and sea" as each "burst into view,
paint[ing] in the flaming colors of a summer sun."

## August 5, 1963

A simple step. Gravity-less. As that of the first woman, or man,
who, one day, long after you or I are gone, will walk on the moon,
just as we've imagined.

A temporary measure – the length of an idea. A wedge. A foot,
say, or an eye.

With which to stay the distance, if only for a moment, between
what is going to happen,
and what, in its going to happen, has already passed.

No wonder each thought is snuffed out so swiftly; that each "shaft
of light" illuminates only a greater darkness; that the foot and the
eye only hover, powerless to descend.

## Firing at the King of Clubs

The promise that the story might be told again, and "from the beginning."

That something will remain – even if unseen – hidden, "at the core."

That the objects of our perception and perception itself will exist, like history, only if perceived.

The promise of things, in short, "mattering."

The compulsion of speech: that words, too, should "matter."

The reason thought gets so often stuck on the tongue, or "misses its mark."

Of the body: the promise of reaching or acquiring what, beyond the body, the body touches upon.

Of the mind: that it will close upon the thought.

Of the moment: that it will close upon itself.

That it will not arrive, in any case, as though independent of probable cause, and a moment too late.

That whatever surfaces – lands "face up" – will not do so only
after the fact.

That everything will exist, like this: as if already played.

That the heart, too, will exist as if six-sided.

Nothing hidden, save the obvious.

A simple decision to let things fall out as they may.

Only afterward, the glancing back – the half recognizing what's not yet fully swung round.

The image – despite certainty – wavering.

A hand could be so easily plunged –.

## Study for the End of the World

When it did begin, it did so both more gradually, and more erratically than the artist had intended.

At the last minute – a malfunctioning of the machine.

A low explosion, before it was expected, then – for a long time – nothing.

The artist approached, tinkered with the wires.

Reflected a little on the single comfort of his trade:

That if the effort should fail, it could – and should – be nothing other than that failed thing.

But the effort did not fail.

There was a stutter. A pop.

A lawn chair jumped, overturning a bucket.

The artist stepped back.

The bucket tripped a wire connected to a tin can and a refrigerator motor.

Then everything – just as the artist had hoped – began to explode before his eyes.

Some people clapped and took photographs.

Then the hoses were turned on, and the sun slipped, glowing strangely in the sky – so that the desert also burned slowly for a while, until darkness fell.

# VII

## Whitewater Draw

Your birthday tomorrow, we drove down with my parents. Got
out as the light was just beginning to fade.

The baby asleep; we shifted her. Gently as we could.
But still, she woke. Cried. Was hushed back to sleep.

My parents walked ahead, toward the look-off; we followed. Took
turns straining through the set of government binoculars mounted
on the boardwalk rail.

When I looked, everything seemed to blink in and out of focus, as
if I was examining a dream I was having about birds, where birds
stood in for something more complex, impossible to define.

You can always feel it, the moment she falls back to sleep, when
you're carrying her: a subtle shift in weight and pressure.

The next morning I wrote on the back of a postcard I'd picked up
years ago – a series of twelve frames by Eadweard Muybridge –
"Horse walking: Free," how we always imagine time like that, as
stalled moments. And although probably it's true that our lives
progress like that in some sense (if only because we think that they
do), really – I wrote – everything is always escaping in between.

My ambition (I don't remember if I wrote this down) is not to
attempt, any longer, to stall time, or second-guess its impulse,
which, for lack of a better word, is "forward" – always past and
through the ambitions of the mind or the body, or whatever seeks
to stop it, or slow it down.

As in: "We didn't know that the birds would fly until they actually did."

Slowly at first, one by one. Then all at once. A dark mass on the horizon, above the irrigated field.

From a distance, they appeared a black swirl; in themselves, a landscape. But when they drew near, they flew singly, or in small groups.

Just as clouds often appear in the distance – dripping with rain that will never actually reach the ground – or mountains appear as a single shape, rather than as the innumerable small gestures made by rock against the pressure of millions of years...

Though even to speak of "millions of years" is a euphemism of sorts, used in order to express...

What exactly?

The way that all things that exist, exist in relation to single moments?

And some sense of the "holy" –?

Of what exists beneath or beyond all of this, somehow?

Of what – beyond a stubborn insistence upon the particular –

simply *exists*. Is eternal. In the way that the sleep of a baby is eternal.

Always, that is, just about to be interrupted.

Like air the beating of wings might, at any moment, redirect.

The whole way home, my mother in the back seat: "We might easily have turned a moment too soon..."

Everything occurs like this – reminding you of something else.

Perhaps "life itself" occurs in this way – as a metaphor for something, which is also itself.

And everything: from what is visible and known – birds, and mountains in the distance, and patterns of wind – to the invisible motives and directions of life and love, is always –

into a moment of which we can only say afterward that it might never have arrived – arriving.

Creating only the impression of stillness, of there having been a moment at all.

Perhaps everything slips – is slipping even now – is utterly free…

But at such a distance, such a distance…

VIII

## Sunrise with Sea Monsters

I want to be a good person.

I want to live my life.

I want to "be reasonable,"
"make compromises" –

though life itself does not.

Though life – in direct opposition to reason –
propels itself only by ramming its head against a wall,
like a blind fish, or a whale.

Until the wall crumbles, and the fish's head is
splintered by light.

. . . . . . .

Within the shape of a human skeleton –
as equally the skeleton of a fish or a bird,
the veins of a leaf, the pattern of pressed rock
or the curve of a shell – is the history of the soul's
attempted flight, simultaneously, in
several opposing directions.

Even now, we must wonder: what is escaping,
what has always escaped?

That groping, wild thing: a spirit one can't master,
a river one can't step into, a ship on the horizon
one can never quite discern…

A letter. Posted to no one. Carried on an invisible ship,
to an un-arrivable shore…

A silence in that letter: what will always remain
unspoken. Between two people who have never
actually communicated...

. . . . . . .

Of course, "One always wants more..."

Even if we accept – exalt, sometimes –
in the incapacities of the word: its maddening
inability to adhere either to subject or object;

in the inevitability with which lines break, meaning
falters or obscures, and poems fail –

exposing at the empty centre the empty centre;

which is to say, of course, after everyone who has
come before – *nothing at all.*

Even if, against both instinct and better judgment,
we insist that, in lieu of any other, better answer,
to point to the empty centre "in a new way" –

acknowledging, therefore, that it has been acknowledged
before – is enough.

. . . . . . .

"One" can only hope, in the end,

that love, if and when it enters, will be different; will be *difference itself.*

That – as opposed to reason, which follows –
it will interrupt. That one will be pulled toward it,
and find it already there.

Obvious and inevitable as a standing wave in a river one can
never actually step into – the reason one can never get across…

Yes. In direct opposition to reason, compromise and every
definition, one wants to be split by love; made monstrous…

. . . . . . .

Because it's just difficult.
All this yes all the time, no all the time.


Still – I know I'll miss it.


Miss banging my head into walls.

Miss chasing myself off precipices out of sheer
enthusiasm for the fact that I can and will fall.


It's that possibility, anyway, by which I am driven –.

The desire (so strong I sometimes confuse it with faith)
to raise myself on two legs, though I've always been
more or less comfortable stumbling around on four.

To makes sudden use of, or abandon altogether, essential organs.

To generate electricity, grow fur; to give birth through my head.

To molt, to lay eggs, to fly –.


Yes, driven. Driven and mad, and – totally uncompromising.

Because ... I'm alive.

Because I'm furious and alive, and split like a rib cage, wanting –
on the one hand – to root, to nest, to shed my skin;

to be propelled by currents, by simple instinct – by the thought,
which never quite becomes a thought

> (Is there a light out there to swim toward?
> Is there a depth? A surfacing?) –

And on the other... To *be* that light. That depth, that surfacing.

To slant in from all directions.

To pierce the waves, touch every point – to *become* the every point
the slanting touches.

To be the simple idea – after the thing, but before the word.

That moment – that pure lucidity –

of apparent, inexpressible, absolutely purposeless joy.

IX

## To be Born is the Supreme Loneliness

To be born is the supreme loneliness.

It is to wake, alone, for the first time; a simple form, startled at its edges.


To be born is to be the first creature.

It is to be the beginning of knowledge, and therefore of desire.


To be born, to *enter,* is to already have required an exit.

It is to be the knot, so to speak, at the end of one's own rope.

The hand placed to the mouth in lieu of the sustaining thing.

It is to be the simple repetition of object and breath; the first,
language-less mouthing at the proffered fist.

It is a supremely lonely thing.


It is not to be companionless – to be without destiny or origin.

It is, instead, to exist "like," or "as," the world into which one is
continuously born.

As the soft hum of the bulb, overhead; as the tread of rubber soles,
back and forth, on the hospital floor.

It is to exist infinitely, and all at once, without limit or end, and,
all the same, "as if" alone, "as if" a single thing...

To be born is to encounter – no, to become this juncture.

To become the fold, as of paper or cloth, where one side in becoming the next conceives of itself as a folded thing.


To be born is to long, suddenly, to be born again.

For the next breath to be the last – the final and sustaining thing.

For the world to occur, again, and all at once.

For light and sound to exist – as they once did – with no difference between them.

For footsteps to travel, no longer back and forth, but – again, and at once – in all directions.


To be born is to discover and become one's own limit.

The body a shorthand – a simple gesture with which one is required to describe,

imperfectly, and only for as long as it holds, the absent centre.

# Ars Poetica

*Written on the Occasion of the Birth of my Daughter*

A poem, like any living thing, should be small; should begin in the mouth.

In perfect darkness. Should unfurl slowly, not knowing what –
until it is that thing – it will be.

That is no doubt the most difficult, perhaps the impossible thing:

For the poem, like any living thing, to contain itself from the beginning.

Everything it will, or might someday become – and not know it,
not even guess.

To be, at first, only small and silent, ignorant of everything, including itself.

To know and not know, at once.

To contain everything it will, or might someday become – but so deeply –
it is impossible even for the poem to understand, or even know it is a poem.

A poem should be sensed. Perhaps by the poet. Perhaps by the reader.

But not by the poem. The poem should not know why or how it
was written.

Like any living thing, it should be ignorant of the answers to
these, and other things.

It should not be a question, in other words, of "mattering" – but of
matter itself.

That is the difficult, perhaps the impossible thing.

For the poem to exist simply – but not to *simply exist.*

Because it is not enough, and never has been, to "simply exist" – and the poem knows it.

Like any living thing, the poem wants more.

The poem is the promise that, in order to exist, it, like any living thing, must want more.

That, though it may start out small, it will not remain that way.

That it may, at any moment, become something new; may grow inside you, may even become you.

That is the most difficult, perhaps the impossible thing.

## "Hunters in the Snow"

In response to the question of figure: ground. Of distance:
touch. Of what cannot be touched: sea, sky.

Every attempt at explanation fails. In this, all things are complicit.
Human being is complicit. In general agreement, that is, with
things as they are – or appear to be.

Yes, to be alive is to be in general agreement with being alive.
It is to accept that, despite or even because of the things we do not
agree with or fail to understand, we must keep on being alive;

that it matters that we do. At least in a small and personal sense, matters.

To be alive is to accept the reduction of all or nearly all terms to
this "small and personal sense." To say "at least" and for it to
mean "enough." *More than enough.* For it to mean "everything."

As it occurs in the moment you are first born, when there is yet no
cause, so that *all* is cause. When to be alive is to *be* cause. Is to respond
to every question with that – simplest – reply.

When living is still just a promise. That there will, and can be, to
all of this, no resolution.

ACKNOWLEDGEMENTS

Versions of some of the poems in this collection appeared previously in the following publications:

"Incident aboard the *Lucky Dragon*: March 1, 1954" in *This Magazine*, July/August 2016. Edited by Dani Couture.

"Hunters in the Snow" in *Mother Mother* 1, no. 1 (2016): 21. Edited by Sheilah Wilson.

"They Will Take My Island" and "Maestro Bartolomé Reconsiders His Creation of Eve" in *Forget Magazine* 8, no. 3 (September 25, 2015). Edited by Kent Bruyneel.

"The Abstract Figure Dreams of His Release" and "Landscape Lessons" (now "Brief Sketches of an Open Field") in *EVENT* 39, no. 2 (Winter 2011).

I'd like to thank those who read this manuscript at various stages of completion: Kate Hall, Annie Guthrie, Sam Ace and John Melillo. I am sincerely grateful for the critical perspectives offered by these readers, as well as for their immense generosity and friendship. Thank you also to my editor, Paul Vermeersch, for his guidance and encouragement. His sustained belief in, enthusiasm for and sharp critical attention to this project has been a continual source of inspiration. Finally, I extend my infinite gratitude to John, and to Olive – for offering me such a perfect description of the world.

The thirteenth-century travelogue *The Description of the World* is more commonly translated into English as *The Travels of Marco Polo.* Polo's travels through Persia, China and Indonesia between 1276 and 1291 were recounted to Rustichello da Pisa, who transcribed them during the time the two spent together in a prison in Genoa. These stories continue to incite debate among historians. Perhaps, some suggest, Polo never travelled to China at all... The origin of the Italian title, *Il Milione,* is also contested. Though some suggest it comes from the Polo family name, *Emilione,* it has also been suggested that the name reflects the opinion (common even at the time of the book's first publication) that the book was filled with "a million" lies. In direct contrast to this conception, however, Rustichello da Pisa sets out the following ambition for the work in his prologue: "We will set down things seen as seen, things heard as heard, so that our book may be an accurate record, free from any sort of fabrication. And all who read the book or hear it will do so with full confidence, because it contains nothing but the truth."

"Brief Sketches of an Open Field": In his influential manifesto, "Projective Verse" (1950), Charles Olson introduces his idea of "composition by field" and declares: "FORM IS NEVER MORE THAN AN EXTENSION OF CONTENT," and "in any given poem always, always one perception must must must MOVE, INSTANTER, ON ANOTHER!"

Maestro Bartolomé was a relatively unknown artist who worked alongside the better-known Fernando Gallego in painting a twenty-six-panel alter for a cathedral in the Castilian province of Salamanca, between 1480 and 1500. The twenty-six panels visualize Christian history from Creation to the Last Judgment. Technological advances in infrared reflectography have revealed stylistic differences between the underdrawings of Bartolomé and Gallego that clearly distinguish the two artists. Most significantly it was found that Bartolomé relied heavily on tracings, and made substantial changes to his compositions as he worked.

In Pablo Neruda's poem "I'm Explaining a Few Things," he speaks of how he once lived in a suburb of Madrid, and then

> one morning all that was burning
> . . . . . . . . . . . . . . . . . . . . . . . . .
> and the blood of children ran through the streets
> without fuss, like children's blood.

The poem concludes with a question and an invitation:

> And you will ask: why doesn't his poetry
> speak of dreams and leaves
> and the great volcanoes of his native land?
> . . . . . . . . . . . . . . . . . . . . . . . . .
> Come and see the blood
> in the streets!

(*Selected Poems*, translated by Nathaniel Tarn, 1970)

"I Give My Powers Away": The title of this poem is inspired by Alfred Lord Tennyson's *In Memoriam*, Section IV:

> To Sleep I give my powers away;
>     My will is bondsman to the dark;
>     I sit within a helmless bark,
> And with my heart I muse and say:
>
> O heart, how fares it with thee now,
>     That thou should fail from thy desire,
>     Who scarcely darest to inquire,
> "What is it makes me beat so low?"

"They Will Take My Island": This title is taken from Arshile Gorky's painting of the same name. The poem was originally written for Paul Vermeersch's project dedicated to collecting poems written in response to Gorky's title and painting.

The titles of all the poems in section IV – "In the Dream, It Shows," "Introduction to Repetition," "The Real is That Which Always Comes Back to the Same Place" and "The Other, Already There" – are borrowed from chapter headings included in Jacques Lacan's *The Four Fundamental Concepts of Psychoanalysis* and his paper "The Direction of the Treatment and the Principles of its Power."

"At Last, the Poet Returns to the City" was originally written for a fall 2012 edition of "The Dictionary Project" – an initiative of poet Lisa O'Neill, in Tucson, Arizona. Participating writers were given two weeks to respond creatively to the prompt of a single word. The word that inspired this poem was *retable*. It also inspired an accompanying piece, which I titled "Apology for a poem not written," and presented alongside the poem. The "Apology" follows:

When I first heard the word *retable* and knew I was going to be responding to the word for "The Dictionary Project" my first impulse was to think about the word itself – then to think about how my initial associations with it corresponded to its definition. My most immediate and obvious association was the word *table* – so I thought about that. Then I thought about the prefix *re-*, which is also, of course, attached to familiar words like *rethink* and *redo*. I thought about how a table might be rethought – repeated in some way – and it occurred to me that the word *table* was in fact already a sort of retabling. That this is the condition of language itself: the substitution of a repeatable sign or symbol for an absolutely unique and unrepeatable "real thing." This put me in mind of Plato and his allegory of the cave, and particularly the part in chapter X, where Socrates says:

> "Take any class of many particulars you please, for instance, if you like, there are many beds and tables.
> "By all means," Glaucon replies.
> "These have ideas, I suppose, underlying them – two in fact: one of the bed, one of the table."

I started to think about the way that language is, in the way that Plato describes here, very much like the dictionary definition of the word *retable*: an alter. The word rests upon the idea, the whole structure assembled very much for the purposes of – and as an act of – faith. Faith that the words we use will cohere with meaning, or, as Plato says in Book X (the same book in which he casts the poets out of his Republic), will "hold fast to truth."

Shortly after I started thinking of the word *retable* in this way, I took a trip to Las Vegas and, driving into the city, I started thinking more about how impossible it is to separate language from image, image from spectacle. I thought about our infatuation with the image, how our worship of it blurs the line between representation and the real.

Then I visited the National Atomic Testing Museum and started to see how all the ideas I had so far come up with for the poem I wanted to write had to do – as everything has to do, perhaps, eventually – with the bomb. Here was pure spectacle: the dramatic split, literalized in the material itself, between the actual and potential power of form.

I started thinking about how Socrates, according to Plato, thought it most expedient to banish the poets from his Republic because – in their presumed refusal to accept, or speak to, things in their "pure" form – they reflected and promoted the very worst, and most conflicted, aspects of human nature. I thought about how the nuclear testing program is really a poetic project in the sense that Plato condemned: an experiment not with the "pure" form of what *is,* but with what – beyond form – can be brought about only through its interaction with the human imagination.

Then, later that day, I learned about the artist Jean Tinguely's project *Study for the End of the World No. 2.* In 1962, at the height of the testing at the Nevada site, Tinguely fashioned an explosive art project, made of junkyard rubble and homemade bombs, took it to the desert outside Las Vegas, and watched it blow. There's a fabulous documentary that chronicles the event, accompanying the footage with ironic commentary like, "Of course, the police are on hand, to make sure that the world blows up in an orderly way."

By now my poem was going to be really big. It was going to include Plato's Republic, the entire city of Las Vegas, the Nevada test site (and the inherent possibility of reading such apocalyptic imagery as *revelation* – I had not, you see, completely forgotten about *the word*), and now it was going to include Jean Tinguely's artistic "imitation" of the end of the world, too.

Then, as if by magic, I stumbled across another piece to the puzzle. In the late 1800s, I learned, when commercial photography was still in its infancy, a fun carnival pastime was gazing into private viewing boxes called Kinetoscopes. There was a general sense of unease about these devices at the time, as it was rumoured they caused dizzy spells, and other "viewer contagions." The language that was used to describe the (potential, unknown) risk Kinetoscopes posed immediately reminded me of the sort of language I'd encountered earlier that day at the National Atomic Testing Museum. It was language that either proposed or summarily dismissed the (potential, unknown) risk of nuclear radiation and that evoked a time before there was any medical proof of the damaging affects of fallout. A time when people still travelled to Las Vegas to watch the explosions from hotel rooftops, when they still ordered atomic cocktails, exclaimed with delight over the "stardust" that turned their skin pink and voted for their favourite Miss Atomic Bomb, dressed in a mushroom cloud, for the Atomic Bomb Beauty Pageant.

The connection between the concern over the potential damage a nuclear bomb could do was interesting to me not because these two perceived threats are in any way comparable in physical terms, but because, once again, and in both cases, it comes back to the relationship between the material world and our projective imaginations. And to these same persistent questions: What are the limits to appearance and perception? What are our responsibilities as witnesses to a world of which we can have only partial knowledge? To what extent are our realities given, and to what extent are they created?

"Flying Home Aboard Enola Gay": This poem was inspired by an article that appeared in the *New York Times* on August 6, 1995, describing the experience of the pilot and commanding officer of the Enola Gay crew, Paul W. Tibbets Jr., and navigator, Theodore J. "Dutch" Van Kirk. Both men recalled what they could of the day. When asked to comment on the moral objections to the bombing of Hiroshima and Nagasaki, Tibbets replied: "No. 1, there is no morality in warfare – forget it."

"Incident Aboard the *Lucky Dragon*: March 1, 1954": The title of this poem refers to the Japanese tuna fishing boat *Daigo Fukuryū Maru* (第五福竜丸) – in English, *No. 5 Lucky Dragon* – which was exposed to nuclear fallout from a test bomb exploded off Bikini Atoll in 1954. The boat's radioman, Aikichi Kuboyama, died seven months later. The quotations in the poem are inspired by crew members' accounts of the incident as reported by Mark Schreiber in *The Japan Times* (March 18, 2012).

"August 5, 1963": In a 1963 radio and television address on the Nuclear Test Ban Treaty, which banned nuclear tests underwater, in the atmosphere and in outer space, John F. Kennedy declared: "Yesterday a shaft of light cut into the darkness." It would not reduce our need for "arms or allies," he said, but it was "an important first step…a step towards reason."

"Firing at the King of Clubs": Harold "Doc" Edgerton was a professor of engineering at MIT. In 1947, he and two colleagues and friends, Kenneth Germeshausen and Herbert Grier, became an incorporated partnership at the request of the Atomic Energy Commission. Known as EG&G, Inc., they designed and operated systems that could time and trigger nuclear bomb tests. Edgerton and his colleagues discovered that in order to capture such a massive release of light in a still photograph, they would have to make exposures of a much shorter duration than had ever been imagined. They invented a rapatronic (for rapid electronic) camera, which – when light hit the photocell of the camera – triggered a mechanism capable of cutting off exposure in two microseconds. Edgerton experimented and demonstrated these new ultra-high-speed techniques by photographing ordinary objects in motion, including human beings, bullets and drops of milk. The title of this poem is borrowed from the title of one of Edgerton's photographs. *Firing at the King of Clubs* depicts a playing card and a bullet. In other images, such as *Cutting the Card Quickly* we see the bullet as it encounters the playing card. *Firing at the King of Clubs* documents a miss – both the bullet and card are visible in this image, side by side.

"Study for the End of the World": Swiss painter and sculptor Jean Tinguely is perhaps best known for his *Homage to New York* (1960), a self-destructing machine, which only partially self-destructed at the Museum of Modern Art before the fire department was called in to extinguish it. His *Study for the End of the World, No. 2* successfully combusted in front of an admiring crowd in the desert outside Las Vegas – the location an "homage," of course, to the nearby Nevada Test Site.

"Whitewater Draw": This wildlife area, located in southeastern Arizona, is a major roost site for sandhill cranes, who migrate to the region annually, sometimes from as far away as Alaska and Siberia.

"Sunrise with Sea Monsters": This title is taken from a J.M.W. Turner painting of the same name. The poem was originally written for Paul Vermeersch's project dedicated to collecting poems written in response to Turner's title and painting.

"Ars Poetica": Édouard Glissant writes, "the logic of what is born is already inscribed in the whole, which has each being arrive at their right place. No being can therefore be self-sufficient, can know himself without knowing – and being born to – the whole… Thus poetry, the domain of metaphor, [is] installed at the heart of knowledge. The logic of what is born is in the end an *Ars poetica*" (*Poetic Intention*. Translated by Nathalie Stephens. Callicoon, NY: Nightboat Books, 1997).

"Hunters in the Snow" refers to the painting by the same title by Pieter Bruegel the Elder from 1565. The painting is one of a series (five of which still survive) depicting different times of year. Inspired by the medieval and early Renaissance tradition of The Labours of the Months, in which twelve scenes depicting rural activities that commonly took place around the year were linked to the signs of the zodiac, the painting can be similarly understood as an expression of humankind's response both to ordering principles and to the unknown.

**Johanna Skibsrud** is the author of two previous collections of poetry, *I Do Not Think that I Could Love a Human Being* and *Late Nights With Wild Cowboys*; two novels, *Quartet for the End of Time* and the 2010 Scotiabank Giller Prize–winning novel *The Sentimentalists*; and the short fiction collection *This Will Be Difficult to Explain and Other Stories*. An Assistant Professor of English at the University of Arizona, Skibsrud and her family divide their time between Tucson and Cape Breton.